Life of
The Loyalists

Rosemary Neering
Stan Garrod
Daniel R. Birch, *Coordinating Editor*

GROWTH
OF A
NATION
SERIES

Fitzhenry and Whiteside

GROWTH OF A NATION SERIES

Life of the Loyalists

© 1995, 1975 Fitzhenry & Whiteside Limited, Markham

ISBN 0-88902-182–1

Printed in Canada

95 96 97 98 99 CR 9 8 7 6 5 4 3 2 1

Authors

Stan Garrod
  Department Head, Collingwood School, Vancouver

Rosemary Neering
  Historian/Writer, Victoria

Series Consultant

Daniel R. Birch
  Vice President and Provost, University of British Columbia

Editors Sheba Meland, Robert Read

Designers Brant Cowie, Darrell McCalla, Raymond Tai

Illustrator J. Merle Smith

Pictures

We would like to thank the staff of the Ontario Provincial Archives, the Nova Scotia Provincial Archives and the United Empire Loyalists' Association of Canada for their help in obtaining material for this book.
Hastings County Historical Society, Belleville, pp. 26, 63 top and centre; Library of Congress, p. 5;
Metropolitan Toronto Library Board, p. 6; Ontario Archives, p. 62 top; Ontariio Ministry of Colleges and Universities, p. 57;
Public Archives of Canada, pp. 7, 26–30, 34 bottom, 41–42, 62 centre and bottom; Royal Ontario Museum, p. 46;
United Empire Loyalists' Association of Canada, p. 34 top.

CANADIAN CATALOGUING IN PUBLICATION DATA

Neering, Rosemary, 1945–
        Life of the loyalists

(Growth of a nation series)
For use in schools.
ISBN 0-88902-182–1

1. United Empire loyalists — Juvenile literature. 2. United States —History — Revolution, 1775–1783 — Juvenile literature.
I. Garrod, Stan. II. Title. III. Series

FC423.N4 1995   971.02'4   C95-930837-7   E277.N4 1995

The *Growth of a Nation* books provide a thematic approach to Canadian History, and complement the texts *Canada: Growth of a Nation* (ISBN 1-55041-194-2) and *Origins: A History of Canada* (ISBN 0-88902-450-2).  Other titles in this series include *Leaving Their Home, Settlement of the West, Life in Acadia, Confederation, Gold Rush, Building a New Life, The School, Life in New France, Energy, Fur Trade, Building of the Railway, The North* and *North West Mounted Police*. For a current list, please write to:

Fitzhenry & Whiteside, 195 Allstate Parkway, Markham, Ontario L3R 4T8

LIFE OF THE LOYALISTS

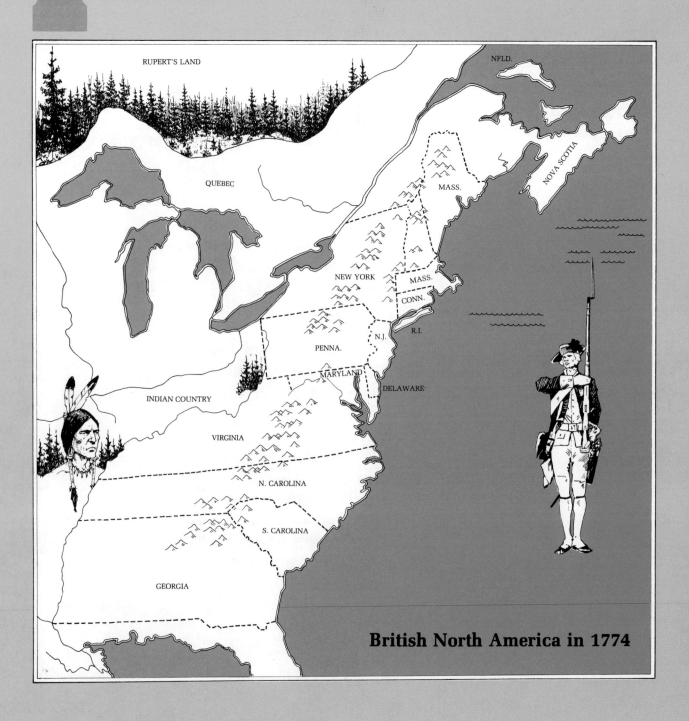

British North America in 1774

1 THE AMERICAN REVOLUTION

Some people disliked the British laws so much that they were very cruel to those who still liked Britain. Here, a crowd is hoisting a Loyalist on a pole.

The people of the British Colonies in America were unhappy. From Quebec and Nova Scotia in the north to Virginia and Georgia in the south, many colonists were complaining. They were upset about having to pay heavy taxes set by the parliament in England. No one should have to pay taxes, the colonists argued, unless they had set the taxes for themselves. What the colonists wanted was the same rights as other Englishmen. In England people could vote for members of parliament who made the taxes. The colonists were not allowed to elect members of parliament.

The most hated of all the tax laws was the Stamp Act. The Stamp Act forced colonists to pay a tax on everyday things like playing cards and newspapers. Newspapers in Halifax, Quebec, Boston and New York refused to pay the tax. Groups of colonists formed to fight the stamp taxes. In New England, a group that called itself The Sons of Liberty was formed. This group forced the British government to change its mind. The Stamp Act was removed but the colonists were still unhappy.

As hated as the Stamp Act was a law that made the colonists pay a tax on imported goods like tea. One day in December of 1773, colonists in Boston—dressed as Indians—sneaked aboard a ship in Boston harbor. They threw 342 cases of tea into the water.

Angry with these acts of protest, the British government passed more laws to punish the colonists. The colonists, in turn, became even more unhappy with the British. They talked about self-government for the colonies. A conference of all the colonies was held in Philadelphia.

Not all of the colonists wanted to split away from England completely. The French Canadians in the Quebec colonies were afraid that the Protestants in New England would not allow religious freedom for Catholics. In all of the colonies, there were many who

At the Boston Tea Party, colonists disguised as Indians dumped cases of tea into the water. Can you think of any reason why the colonists dressed up as Indians?

were against independence from England. When the Declaration of Independence was signed in Philadelphia on July 4, 1776, the Quebec, Nova Scotia, Saint John's Island, and New York colonies refused to sign.

Even before the Declaration of Independence was written, fighting had started between the colonists in New England and the British troops. The Declaration of Independence created a new country, the republic of the United States of America. The twelve colonies who signed said that they wanted to rule themselves. They did not want to be ruled by the King of England.

However, Britain was not willing to let the colonies go. Armies were sent to fight against the colonists who wanted independence. The American Revolution had begun.

1. Make a list of the thirteen North-American British colonies of 1775. Are all of these colonies states in the United States of America today?
2. Why, do you think, did the colonies in what is now Canada not join the American Revolution?
3. Find out more about the American Revolution.

The war did not go well for the British. At Saratoga, General Burgoyne had to surrender his army of 6,000 men to the American revolutionaries.

Not everybody in the colonies wanted to be independent of Britain. There were people who wanted to be ruled by the King of England even in the colonies that signed the Declaration of Independence. Some colonists thought that revolution was bad. They felt that no one should ever rebel against the King. Others did not want to lose the advantages of being British. Yet others thought the rebels—or patriots, as they called themselves—were violent men who could not be trusted.

The people who opposed the revolution were called Loyalists or Tories. They called themselves Loyalists. The rebels called them Tories, a word used to describe conservative politicians who resisted change. It is thought that as many as one-third of the people living in the rebel colonies were Loyalists.

1. What does the word "loyal" mean? How did the Loyalists get their name?
2. Do we still use the word "Tory"? What does it mean today?
3. The British called the people who wanted independence "rebels". They called themselves "patriots". Can you explain why? What is the difference in the meaning between these two words?

2 AT HOME ON THE HUDSON

Jake Booth came pounding down the dusty Hudson Valley road toward his house.

"Dad," he started yelling before he reached the door, "Dad, there's a gang of rebels on the way. They say they're going to get you and all the Tories they can find. They said I'd better get out of the way quick before they decide to tar and feather me too. What are we going to do?"

Richard Booth came dashing out of the house. "Don't just stand around there, son," he shouted. "Get out the horses and we'll ride on out somewhere where they can't find us."

"What about Mom and Samuel?"

"They'll be all right. Even the rebels wouldn't harm a woman. Your brother's too young for them to worry about."

Father and son ran to the stable. But they were too late. As they came out with the horses, a gang of men blocked their path. One of them got off his horse and slowly walked up to Richard Booth, swinging a whip in his hand.

"Just where do you think you're going, Mister Tory?" he asked. "Think you'll to get away from us? Is he going to get away, boys?"

"No," shouted the rest of the gang. "We got us a Loyalist and he's going to pay for it," said one of them.

"We got some nice hot tar all set down at the crossroads," said another. "So why don't you come with us? Get on your horse, you too, boy. See what happens to Americans who don't fight for us!" He took the reins of the two horses and the Booths were led off in the middle of the group.

At the crossroads, a pot of black tar hung over a low fire. The men grabbed Richard Booth and began to

tear off his clothes. Jake flung himself at them, screaming and begging them to let go of his father.

"Back off boy," said one of them, roughly, "or you'll be getting it too." He pushed Jake aside.

It was over in a few minutes. The men smeared the thick black tar all over Richard Booth, then they pushed handfuls of feathers into the tar; finally, they stepped back to admire their handiwork.

"Not bad," said one, bursting into laughter. "Maybe that will teach you what happens to Tories around here. Chicken feathers for a cowardly King's man! Where's your King to help you now? We don't want your kind of people around here. Clear out and take your family with you! Next time we come we'll take you to jail and it will be the hangman's noose for you."

Jake and his father walked back home, leading the horses behind them. Jake kept looking sideways at his father. As they came into the farmyard, he could stand it no longer. He broke into giggles and pointed at the black tar all speckled with white feathers. His father reached out and with one tarry hand slapped Jake a-cross the face.

"That'll teach you to laugh. Get inside and don't let me see you again today." He stalked off toward the barn, chicken feathers making a path behind him.

1. The group of men who tarred and feathered Richard Booth called him a "Tory" and a "Loyalist". What do these words mean?
2. Why did the men tar and feather Richard Booth? How would you feel if you were being tarred and feathered? Do you think this is a good form of punishment? Why or why not?
3. The story doesn't tell us how Jake's father got rid of the tar and the feathers. Try to think of a way.

Jake woke up during the night. He could hear his parents argue in the kitchen. He slipped downstairs and stood behind the kitchen door.

" . . . not going to be chased out of here by a bunch of no-good ruffians," Richard Booth was saying. "I put my whole life into this farm. Nobody is going to push me off. I'm not moving."

"Then we'll go without you," said Mary Booth. "I'm not staying here to see you thrown into jail. How would we run the farm without you? And who knows what would happen to the boys?

"We can start a new life somewhere else. I hear the King has promised free land to all the American loyalists. You can be as stubborn as you like, Dick Booth, but I'm leaving and the boys are going with me."

Jake's father sighed. He sat down heavily at the table.

"I guess you're right. Not much point in staying here. Maybe we can get some land in Nova Scotia or Quebec."

Jake could stand it no longer. "Why do we have to go?" he cried, as he threw himself through the doorway. "Why can't we join the rebels? That would make them happy, wouldn't it? Isn't that what they want — for all Americans to be rebels?"

"It's too late for that, son. We made our choice five years ago. We're the King's men and always will be. We're not rebels. We never could be. No one has the right to fight against his King. You can't change what you believe in, just because your side is losing. Remember that, Jake."

Booth turned to his wife. "We'll be leaving as soon as possible. We'll head for the city of New York, the British troops are still there; they'll look after us. Pack up enough food to keep us for a week, and clothes for Samuel and yourself. Jake, you pack your own things. Don't take much. We'll be traveling light and fast."

1. Do you think the Booths did the right thing when they decided to leave? What else could they have done?

2. Can you think of a recent example when Americans left their country to come to Canada, rather than fight in a war they didn't believe in?

3. Do you think the Booths could call themselves "Americans" and still be loyal to the British King? What does the term "American" mean? Are Canadians Americans?

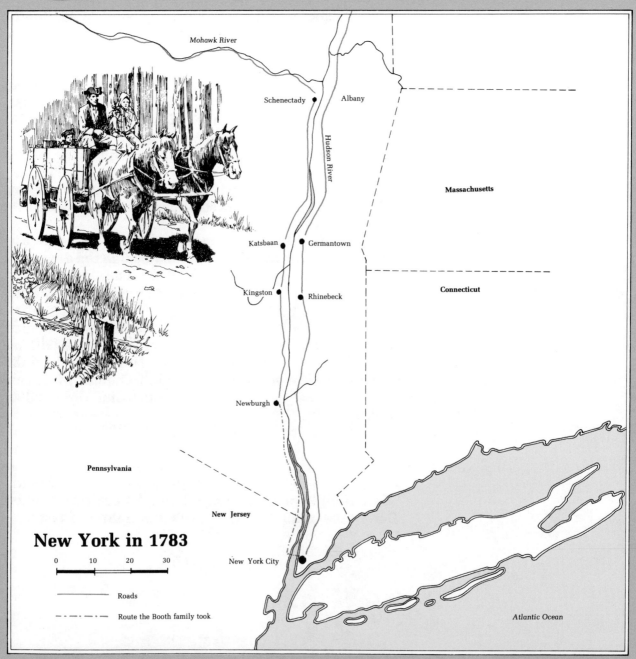

New York in 1783

0   10   20   30

Roads

Route the Booth family took

Mohawk River

Schenectady   Albany

Hudson River

Massachusetts

Katsbaan   Germantown

Kingston   Rhinebeck

Connecticut

Newburgh

Pennsylvania

New Jersey

New York City

Atlantic Ocean

1. How far is it from Newburgh to New York City?
2. What do the names of the towns on the map tell you about the people who settled along the Hudson River valley?

3
FLIGHT TO NEW YORK

The crying of his younger brother startled Jake from his sleep. The wagon was still traveling south from Newburgh along the Hudson River towards New York City. The Booth family had been on the road for two days.

Now it was dark. The wagon stopped. Richard Booth jumped down onto the road. "I'll just go into this inn and see if we can get a hot meal here," he said. He walked toward the lighted windows ahead. Jake watched him open the door. Two minutes passed.

Suddenly, the door flew open and Booth came dashing out, a crowd of men chasing after him.

"Tory," they yelled, "get the Tory! Run him down! String him up!"

Booth shouted to his wife, "Whip up the horses, I'll jump aboard!"

Mary Booth grabbed the reins and slapped them down on the backs of the horses. They broke into a trot, then into a gallop. As they raced by the inn, Booth seized the side of the wagon and swung himself up. The men from the inn were soon left behind.

"That was a narrow escape," gasped Booth. "Don't know how they knew I was a Loyalist. I barely had time to ask if we could get a meal, when they were out of their seats and after me. We'll have to make do with the bread and cheese we have with us. We're not stopping again until we get to the city."

The wagon jogged on through the night, past lonely farmhouses and through small villages. Sometimes, only the noise of the horses' hooves striking the hard road could be heard.

As the sun rose, Jake climbed up to sit beside his father. "Where are we?" he asked.

"Getting pretty close now," said Booth." Just have to cross the river and we'll be safe in the city."

The wagon rolled up to the river bank. Jake's father called to a man who stood at the edge of the water. "Where can we find a boat that will take us across to the city?"

"On down there a piece," he called back.

14

The Booth family continued along the river. A short distance ahead, they saw a ferry. A tall thin man stood beside it, chewing on a piece of grass.

"Will you take us across?" Jake's father asked.

"Reckon so. Horses will have to swim on behind, though. No room for them in the boat." He spat into the water. "You folks Tories?"

"Yes."

"Lots like you in the city. Don't matter none to me. Loyalists, rebels, old George, young George, red coats, blue coats, it's all the same to me.

"I never had anything to do with that sort of nonsense. I just run my boat. S'long as I make enough money to feed myself and my family, that's all I care about."

He pushed the boat off the shore. The horses, tied to the stern, swam slowly after the ferry. "You'll have to grab an oar, Mister; you too, young fellow. My helper went off a year ago to join the rebels down Philadelphia way. Ain't heard from him since. The silly fool probably got himself killed."

At the far shore, the Booths got out and were on the road again. There were more buildings along the way—houses, inns and churches. As they came into the city of New York, Jake stared at the people bustling back and forth. He was amazed to see the sailing ships on the river, and the red coats of the British soldiers.

This then was New York! Here the Booths would stay until they could travel north to Quebec.

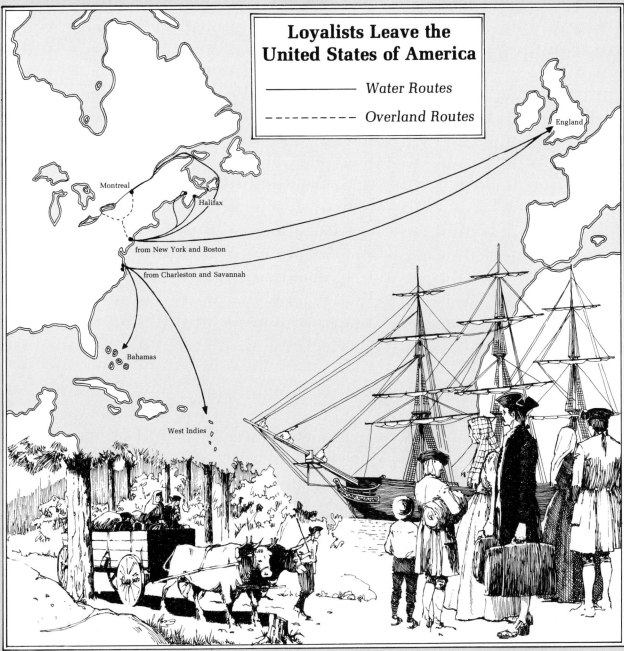

Loyalists Leave the
United States of America

Water Routes

Overland Routes

Montreal

Halifax

from New York and Boston

from Charleston and Savannah

England

Bahamas

West Indies

4

Loyalist Settlement in Canada

Areas settled by Loyalists

Six Nations Reserve

Quebec

Montreal

Cornwall

Kingston

York

Niagara

Windsor

Saint John

Halifax

Shelburne

Atlantic Ocean

1. What do all the areas settled by the Loyalists have in common? Why, do you think, was this important in 1783?
2. Look at your atlas. Are all the areas settled by Loyalists important cities today?

4 LOYALISTS LEAVE THE UNITED STATES

The war went on for six years. By 1782, the British soldiers had been pushed back to New York. A year later, a treaty was signed, giving the United States of America their independence.

What could the Loyalists do now? Most of the states had already passed laws, forbidding anyone who had helped the British to own property or to vote. Anyone who did could be thrown into jail.

People who had fought neither for the revolution nor for the British could stay in the United States. But most of those who had joined the British army or helped the British in some other way did not want to stay.

Where could they go? Some went back to Great Britain. Others went to the West Indies. Most, almost 40,000 Loyalists, came north to Canada.

Many of them went to Nova Scotia. They settled at the new town of Shelburne, near Halifax, or along the St. John River and at other places along the water. Soon, the new colony of New Brunswick was created for them.

There were many professional people among the Loyalists who came to the Maritimes. They had worked as lawyers, judges, doctors and businessmen in the cities of the Thirteen Colonies. They brought with them many of their possessions. Some, who had to farm to make a living in the new land, found their new life very difficult.

The Loyalists who went to settle in what is now Ontario were mostly farmers and tradesmen. Many of them were soldiers who had fought for the British in the war.

In 1783, this area was still a part of Quebec. It was not until 1792 that Quebec was split into the new colonies of Upper Canada and Lower Canada.

1. Imagine you are the governor of Nova Scotia and are told that 35,000 people will come to settle in your area. What would you do to prepare for their arrival? Where would you house the Loyalists? How would you feed them? What kind of food would you give them and where would you get it?

2. If you were a Loyalist who had to leave the United States in 1783, where would you have gone? Why?

3. Many of the people who stayed loyal to Britain in the revolution, were not British subjects but settlers who had come to America from Germany, Holland, Scandinavia and other European countries. Can you think of reasons why they would have wanted the colonies to remain under British rule?

UNITED EMPIRE LOYALISTS

The loyalists are sometimes known as the "United Empire Loyalists." This name came into use after 1789, when Lord Dorchester, Governor-General of British North America, suggested that he put "a marke of Honour upon those families who had adhered to the Unity of the Empire and joined the Royal Standard in America before the Treaty of Separation in 1783." A list of these families was drawn up and anyone whose name was on the list, could put the initials U.E. after his or her name.

What was the British Empire? What do you think Lord Dorchester meant by "the Unity of the Empire"? If you do not understand the words he used, look them up in a dictionary.

Sorel

Halifax

**Sea Route
from New York
to Sorel, Quebec**

New York

Atlantic Ocean

5 ON TO SOREL

"The war is over! The war is over!" The man ran shouting past the inn where Jake and his family had been staying since coming to New York a year earlier.

"What happened?" Jake yelled. But no one in the crowd would stop to tell him. At last, his father came home.

"Dad, what happened? What did they say?"

"The governor read us the proclamation. The war is over and a treaty has been signed. The rebels have won. We're now standing on the soil of the United States of America."

"And we'll no longer pay our taxes to King George," interrupted a young man. "The redcoats can go home and you Tories can find somewhere else to live."

Jake turned to his father. "Does that mean we have to leave here, Dad?"

"Yes. We'll be taking a ship to Quebec as soon as we can. I hear they've promised every Loyalist who wants it at least one hundred acres of land free. That'll give us a new start."

The news of the Peace of Paris reached America in March of 1783, but it was not until July 4 that the Booths left New York aboard the ship *Camel*, bound for Quebec. Seven other ships crowded with Loyalists left New York that week, on their way to Canada.

The weather quickly turned stormy, and the 106 Loyalists who were aboard huddled below deck, out of the wind and the rain. After fifteen days at sea, they sailed into Halifax Harbor to take on water and other supplies.

"Many a Loyalist is living here now," an old man told Jake, as they looked at the shoreline of Nova Scotia. "Nothing but trees there, when they arrived. Look at it now — towns, farms and houses."

Jake looked doubtfully at the land. Besides Halifax, a town that had been settled before the Loyalists arrived, all he could see were trees and a few houses.

Their ship sailed along the coast, around Cape Breton Island. The air turned colder and fog closed in. Jake could see only grey mist. The wind died down and the sails hung slack.

"Are we lost?" Jake whimpered. "Will the wind come back?"

"In time," a soldier told him, "in time."

The wind came back but brought yet another storm, rocking the boat from side to side. The Loyalists sat uneasily below deck, their faces grey. "Had a ship sink under me in just such a storm," one man said. The others just glared at him.

As they rounded the Gaspé Peninsula and sailed into the Gulf of St. Lawrence, the sun came through and the weather turned fine again. Now a new problem worried the Loyalists. Half the children on board had broken out in red spots. "It's the measles or the small-pox," said the ship's doctor.

Jake and his family moved their belongings out on deck. "Let's sleep here and we'll stay well," said Mary Booth. "Down below we'll catch the sickness for sure."

On and on they sailed, passing farmhouses and churches, barns and roads. Sometimes a child would wave to them from the riverbank.

After five weeks, they saw a town ahead built high on a cliff above the river. There was a walled fort beside it. Here, the Loyalist ships dropped anchor.

They did not stay long at Quebec, but were immediately loaded onto wagons and taken to the Seigneury of Sorel, where hundreds of other Loyalists were already camped. They would wait there until the next spring, while the lands further up the St. Lawrence River were being surveyed. Then they would move upstream to their new homes.

1. How do you think the Booths and other Loyalists felt when they heard the war was definitely lost? Pretend you are Jake Booth. Write a letter to a friend in Newburgh, telling him how you feel and where you are going.

2. The boat that carried the Booth family could not go all the way from Halifax to Sorel without stopping to pick up supplies. What kind of supplies would they be? Look at an atlas and find places where they might have stopped.

3. Name the city with the fortress on the hill that Jake saw. Do you think the ship would have stopped there?

4. Using your atlas, list the interesting sights Jake would have seen during his boat trip from New York to Sorel. Make sure they are things he could see.

6
THE SOREL CAMP

It was raining again. It had started the day after the Loyalists arrived at Sorel, and had not stopped since.

"I hate November and I hate Quebec and I wish I were back home," thought Jake, as he walked past the grey tents and huts of the Loyalist camp. He angrily kicked a rock that lay in his path. Pain shot through his foot. He clutched his toe and hopped around in a circle, trying not to cry.

"That was dumb," a calm voice said behind him. He swung around. A girl, about his own age, had been watching him.

"Who are you?" asked Jake.

"I am Elizabeth McDonnell," answered the girl.

"I didn't see you on the boat."

"Oh, we've been here for months and months. My Mom and sister and brother and I came from Vermont by cart last summer. It was really exciting. We got chased by rebels and had to hide in a cornfield one whole day until it got dark, and we could move on."

"Where was your Dad?"

"In the army, fighting for the King. He came down from Quebec and met us at Isle aux Noix on Lake Champlain. Then we came here by boat."

"The rebels tarred and feathered my father," said Jake, "and we got caught in a really bad storm at sea."

"That's nothing. See that man over there in the red cap? He was in prison for ages for being a Loyalist. One night, the jailkeeper was feeling happy because the rebels had won a big battle. He got drunk and forgot to lock the cell door. The man escaped and ran away. He came here and is now going to Cataraqui with us."

Elizabeth walked towards Jake. "Do you want to go down to the river?" she asked. "I can show you where they bring in the food for us, by boat. Do you know what you get to eat here? Peas and pork for breakfast, pork and peas for dinner and pork or peas for supper!"

They laughed and suddenly Jake's toe didn't hurt quite as much. Even the rain didn't seem quite as wet.

"Race you to the river," shouted Jake and he and Elizabeth splashed off through the mud.

Find Vermont, Lake Champlain, Isle aux Noix and Sorel on a map. Trace the route you think the McDonnells would have taken to Sorel from Vermont.

THE LOYALIST LIST

To His Excellency General Haldimand, Governor-General and Commander in Chief:

The Loyalists, going to form a settlement at Cataraqui, ask:

That *boards, nails and shingles be given to each Loyalist family so that they may build houses and other buildings; that eighty squares of window glass also be given each family.*

That *arms, ammunition and one ax be given to each male, aged fourteen or more.*

That *the following things be given to each family:*
One plow shear and coulter
Leather for horse collars
Two spades
Three iron wedges
Fifteen iron harrow teeth
Three hoes
One inch and one half-inch auger
Three chisels
One gouge
Three gimblets
One hand saw and files
One nail hammer
One drawing knife
One frow for splitting shingles
Two scythes and one sickle
One broad ax

That *one grindstone be given for every three families.*

That *one year's clothing be given to each family.*

That *two years' provisions be given to each family, enough according to their number and age.*

That *two horses, two cows and six sheep be delivered at Cataraqui for each family.*

That *seeds of different kinds such as wheat, Indian corn, peas, oats, potatoes and flax be given to each family.*

That *one blacksmith be established in each township.*

—adapted from the Loyalist Petition
to Governor Haldimand, written at Sorel,
January, 1784.

1. Make a list of the things the Loyalists asked for. Write down what you think each item would have been used for. If you do not understand some of the words, look them up in the glossary at the back of the book.

2. What foods could you get from the seeds and from the animals the Loyalists asked for?

3. Would the things on this list give them what they needed to live? What else might they need? Where and how could they get these other things?

4. Governor Haldimand gave the Loyalists food for three years, axes, guns, hoes, seeds and clothing. Are these the things you would have chosen, if you could not have had everything you asked for? If you could take to Cataraqui only ten of the items listed, which ten would you choose?

General Sir Frederick Haldimand

Mother and daughter spinning in the kitchen. How does the spinning wheel work? How will they make cloth from the spun yarn?

7 SOREL TO CATARAQUI

The Loyalist camp at Johnstown. What are the Loyalists doing while waiting to go to their land? Where is Johnstown?

It was a cold winter. By Christmas, there was a foot of snow on the ground. More fell in January. The Loyalists shivered in their leaking huts and tents.

The snow was slow to melt. Then, at last, spring came, and the ground thawed. Every day, Jake and Elizabeth went down to the river to look out for the boats.

By mid-May, they had not yet arrived. "I hear they will never come," said one man. "They'll be here tomorrow," said another.

One night, a whisper ran through the camp. "The boats are on their way! We'll be leaving the day after tomorrow."

No one believed it at first. But the next day, a fleet of large flat-bottomed bateaux sailed into the harbor. Suddenly the camp was alive. The Loyalists lined up for new clothes, issued by the government. They found out in which bateau they would travel. They packed up their belongings and got ready to leave Sorel.

The Booths and McDonnells were on the same bateau. "Not sorry to leave this place," Booth muttered as they pulled away from the dock. "Nor I," said McDonnell. "Let's hope Cataraqui is a better place."

The bateaux were poled out into the river, and the boatmen hoisted the sails. The strong wind sent them upriver, past farms and houses, churches and fields. At Montreal they stopped to pick up supplies. Then they set out across the clear blue waters of Lake St. Louis.

Ahead were the boiling Cascades Rapids. Elizabeth turned pale when she saw the rough water. "How will we sail across that?" she asked.

One of the boatmen turned to her and smiled. "You will get out here and go by cart to where the rough water ends," he said. "We will take the bateaux through the rapids with our poles."

"Can I stay in the boat?" Jake shouted. "Please, I won't be any trouble. May I stay?"

The boatman looked doubtful. "Well," he said, "You may, if your father says it's all right."

"Dad, can I, please? Please?"

"Will the boy be safe?" asked Jake's father.

"Oh, he'll be safe enough. He might get a little frightened."

"All right, Jake, you can stay."

"Then I'm staying too," announced Elizabeth.

"You can't," Jake said. "You're a girl and stuff like this is too dangerous for girls."

Elizabeth folded her arms in front of her. "I'm staying; girls can do anything boys can do and a lot more besides." She glared at Jake. "You can't bake bread or spin yarn, I bet!"

The boatman laughed. "Let them both stay. They'll be all right," he said.

The boat nosed into a dock at the foot of the rapids. As the passengers got out, the men lowered the sails and unloaded most of the baggage. Then they

These Loyalists are shown camping beside the St. Lawrence on their way up the river in 1784. Who can you see in the picture besides the Loyalists?

turned the boat back into the foaming water, digging their long poles into the river bed. "Hold it, keep close to shore," yelled one of them, as the boat started to move downstream. "Dig in that pole!" shouted another.

As the boat knifed into a whirlpool, water sprayed its bow. Although Elizabeth and Jake ducked, they were not fast enough. Both got drenched.

"Hold on, *mes enfants*," shouted one of the boatmen. "*Alors*, here we go!" The men leaned hard against their poles. The boat nosed through the swirling waters, slowly moving upstream, swaying back and forth and fighting the river all the way. At last, calm waters appeared ahead. In another few minutes, they were clear of the rapids.

The boatmen let out a cheer. "*Bien*, you are all right, *eh*?" said one of them to the children. "There are your parents now."

The other passengers stood on the riverbank with the baggage, as the bateau put into shore to pick them up.

"You look a little wet," said McDonnell with a smile. "Rough trip?"

Jake and Elizabeth looked at each other and grinned. "No," they said together, "it was easy."

The brigade of bateaux continued upriver. Every night the boatmen poled into shore and helped all the passengers to climb out. At first, it was exciting to pitch tents in different places and eat supper beside a campfire. But as days turned into weeks, everyone got tired of the trip. Always the same things to see: trees, trees and more trees, with once in a while a cabin along the riverside.

Nothing much to do, except sit and watch the boatmen move the bateau slowly along. Always the same to eat: pork and more pork, peas and more peas.

They had been moving upstream for almost four weeks. Then they passed a large tent camp where the Loyalists who had come to take up land near Johnstown were staying.

Soon the river widened. There were islands along the shore. On the twenty-sixth day, they saw the buildings of Fort Frederick and Cataraqui. The boats pulled into shore. The Loyalists had finally arrived at their new home.

1. One of the boatmen spoke in a language other than English. What was it? Why would he have used it? What is the difference between the words "bateau" and "bateaux"? What language are these words? What do they mean in English?

2. The Loyalists were not the first people to live near Cataraqui. Who lived there before them? Think of two groups of people. Here is a clue: Fort Frederick was once called *Fort Frontenac.*

3. You and a Loyalist friend have left your homes in the new United States months ago. You have not yet reached your new homes. Tell each other about your hopes and fears as you travel along on the river.

This is what the Loyalists saw when they arrived at Cataraqui in 1784. Who do you think was living in these buildings?

DISTRIBUTION OF CLOTHING TO THE REFUGEE LOYALISTS AS APPROVED BY GENERAL HALDIMAND

To Each Man or Boy above Ten Years of Age	Coats		1
	Waistcoats		1
	Breeches	Pairs	1
	Hat		1
	Shirts (or 3½ Yards Linen)		1
	Leggings	Pairs	1
	Stockings	Pairs	1
	Blanket		1
	Shoe Soles	Pairs	1
To Each Woman or Girl above Ten Years of Age	Woollen Cloth	Yards	2
	Linen Cloth	Yards	4
	Stockings	Pairs	1
	Blanket		1
	Shoe Soles	Pairs	1
To Each Child under Ten Years of Age	Woollen Cloth	Yards	1
	Linen Cloth	Yards	2
	Stockings	Pairs	1
	Blanket (between two)		1
	Shoe Soles	Pairs	1

Also issued: One tent for every five persons, and one camp kettle for each tent.

1. Look carefully at the one list of clothes for men and boys and the other one for women and girls. What is the difference between them? Why, do you think, was there a difference in the two lists?

2. If you were given the lengths of material shown to dress your children, what type of clothing would you make? How would you find out how much was needed to make each article? How would the Loyalist women have found out?

3. How big, do you think, was the average Loyalist family? Is there anything on the list that would help you answer this question?

Sorel to Kingston

REPORT OF THE WORKS THAT HAVE BEEN COMPLETED FOR THE LOYALISTS AT CATARAQUI DURING THE WINTER

Cataraqui, 14th June, 1784

Wharf sunk and filled with Stone to the Level of the Water.

Saw Mill Complete.

Grist Mill now in Hand and Somewhat Advanced.

Captain Brant's House, 40 foot in Front by 30 foot in Depth and One Story and a Half, Complete.

Miss Molly Brant's House, nearly Complete.

Navy Store 50 foot by 25 foot, Built but not Finished.

Timber Squared 9,000 Feet Cubic.

Round Logs, 1,000.

Building Timber, 50 Pieces.

1. How many buildings were built during the winter of 1783-84? What kind of buildings were they?
2. What were the timber and the round logs used for?
3. Although a sawmill had been built at Cataraqui, many of the Loyalists who lived in nearby townships used logs rather than sawn planks to build their cabins. Why do you think this happened? Why would the Loyalists need a saw mill?

8 THE LOYALIST INDIANS

When Europeans first came to North America, they made friends with the Indians who lived nearby. Several powerful tribes, the Mohawks, the Iroquois, the Mohicans and the Hurons, took part in the French-English wars and fought side by side with either French or British soldiers. After the English defeated the French in 1760, most of the Indians came over to the British side.

When the American Revolution began, those Indian tribes fought with the British troops in the battles along the frontier. The most important of these were five of the six tribes that made up the Six Nations Confederacy—the Mohawks, Oneidas, Cayugas, Onondagas and the Tuscaroras. Only the Senecas supported the rebels.

After the war, most of the Indian tribes left the United States. Some stayed at Cataraqui but most of them moved on to an area near the Grand River. Like other Loyalists, they were given land grants. The land, six miles wide on both sides of the river, along its entire length, was given to the Five Nations.

One of the most important leaders of the Indian Loyalists was Captain Joseph Brant, a Mohawk chief. Brant had helped in missionary work among the Indians before the war. Now he decided to live the rest of his life like an English gentleman. He built a large house near what is now Burlington, Ontario, kept servants and Negro slaves and wore fine English clothing.

Some of Brant's children decided to live as he did. Others preferred the traditional Indian life. His son Isaac disagreed with his father's way of life and fought bitterly with him. In the final quarrel, Brant killed his son.

After Joseph Brant's death, his wife moved out of the big house. She preferred to be among her own people, beside the Grand River.

Joseph Brant.

Joseph Brant and the Mohawks arrive at Grand River.

1. Do the Five Nations still live beside the Grand River? Try to find out what happened to the lands they were given by the government.

2. The Indians lived in North America long before Europeans arrived. It could be said they owned all the land. How, then could the British give land to the Indians? Did the British own the land?

3. Find the Grand River on a map of Ontario. Can you see place names that tell you Loyalist Indians had settled there?

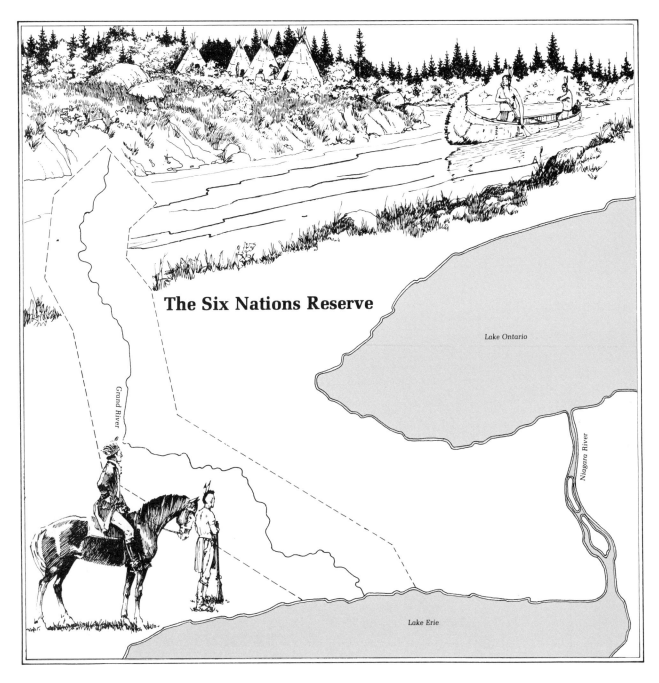

The Six Nations Reserve

Lake Ontario

Niagara River

Grand River

Lake Erie

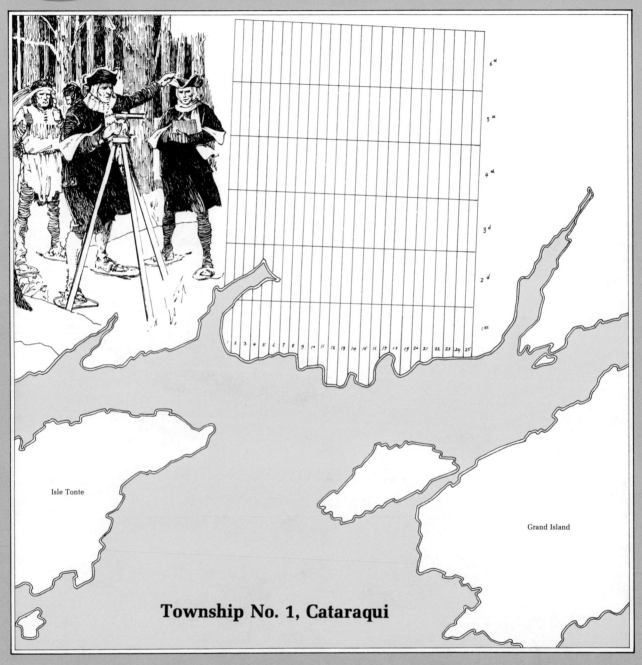

6 th

5 th

4 th

3 d

2 d

1 st.

1 2 3 4 5 6 7 8 9 10 11 12 13 14 15 16 17 18 19 20 21 22 23 24 25

Isle Tonte

Grand Island

Township No. 1, Cataraqui

9 SURVEYING THE LOYALIST LAND GRANTS

The land given to the Loyalists lay along the north shore of the St. Lawrence River, between what are now Cornwall and Kingston. There were no maps to show them where their slice of land was.

In 1783, before the settlers left Sorel, the British governor had ordered a survey of the area. Trees and brush covered the land and surveyors had little time to mark out each individual grant before the settlers came. Instead, the surveyors decided to mark the outer edges of each township and divide each township into concessions.

Surveys of five townships were made in the Cataraqui—Bay of Quinte area. The first survey of Township No. 1, called Kingston, marked the location of the fort, the site for a town and the block of lots granted to the settlers.

As the Loyalists arrived and claimed and cleared their land, a second and more accurate survey was made. Then each owner registered his title to the farm at a Land Registry Office.

THE SURVEYING PARTY:

There were between six to twelve men in a surveying party.

The **surveyor**, in charge of the group, drew maps and made reports to the government.

The **deputy surveyor** was responsible for the rest of the men in the party. He gave them their equipment, food and pay.

He received one-and-a-half shillings per day, per man. Out of this, he had to buy one-and-a-half pounds of flour, twelve ounces of pork and half-a-pint of peas, to feed each man. Sometimes the survey party caught fish or shot game, to add to their meals of salt pork, pea soup and bread.

The **axemen** cleared the brush along the survey path. They were paid one-sixth of a shilling a day. Indians were often employed as axemen.

The **chainmen** used steel chains to measure distances. They earned two-and-a-half shillings a day.

The **picketmen** drove in stakes to mark the edge of each lot.

THE SURVEYING INSTRUMENTS:
Circumferentor, Sextant, Surveyor's Chain

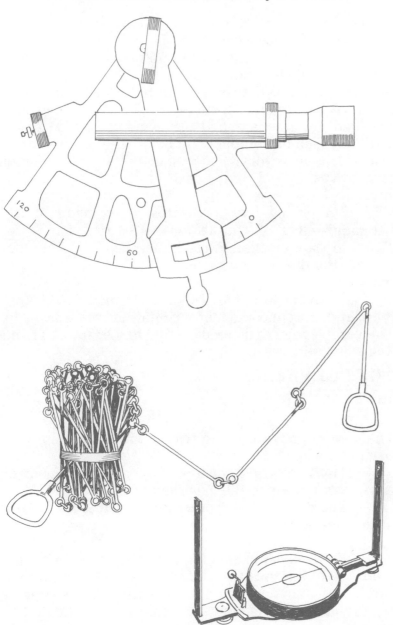

A sextant was used to find the exact location of the place to be surveyed.

A steel chain, 66 feet long, consisting of one hundred links, was used to measure distances.

A magnetic compass, called a circumfrentor, showed the direction.

HOW THE SURVEYING WAS DONE:

The surveyor first chose a baseline for the township to be surveyed. Then he took a reading with his sextant to find the exact location of one end of the baseline. He set his circumfrentor on a stump or flat rock, close to the start of the baseline.

The axemen cleared any trees that were in the way of the line.

A picketman drove in one stake at the starting point of the baseline.

One of the chainmen held the first link of the chain; his partner walked along with the other end of the chain until it was stretched tight. A second picketman drove in a second stake at this point.

The surveyor used his compass to look from the first stake to the second, to make sure his line was straight. Then he repeated the whole process.

At the end of 30 chains, a picketman drove in a large stake, to show the edge of the lot.

The basic unit of Loyalist land was a lot of 200 acres. Each lot was 30 chains wide and 68 chains deep. Each row of 24 lots was a concession. A township was usually 24 lots wide and six concessions deep. Every four or six lots, a road allowance of one chain was set aside, and another road allowance was made after each two concessions.

Once the whole township was surveyed, each settler received a piece of paper showing the location of his grant. On it, it might say: "Township No. 1, Concession 3, Lot 12."

1. Chainmen were paid more than axemen. Why?
2. Find out more about how sextants and circumferentors work.
3. How big was a township?
4. Contact the public works department where you live, and find out how surveying is done now.

DRAWING LOTS

Loyalists drawing lots for their land.

At the Cataraqui townsite, the Loyalists crowded around a man with a hat in his hand. Beside him was a second man who held a large sheet of paper.

The man with the hat called for silence. "Now," he yelled out, "every man here is entitled to 100 acres of free land and 50 more acres for every person in his family. Each man will now draw for his land.

"When I call your name, come up here and pull a piece of paper from this hat. This gentleman on my left will write down your name beside the description of your land. Then he will show you the location of your land on the map. Any questions?"

"What if we don't like the land we draw?" shouted one of the Loyalists.

"You're welcome to trade it with someone else or even sell it, if you can. If you can't, you'll just have to keep what you draw. There will be no second chances."

The man began to call out names. One by one, the Loyalists stepped forward to draw for their land.

"Simon McDonnell," then, a few minutes later, "Richard Booth."

Elizabeth and Jake waited anxiously. "Is our land close to McDonnell's?" Jake asked his father. "Will we be neighbors?"

Before Booth could answer, McDonnell came back. "Managed to trade," he said. "I'm next to you now, back on the third concession. We can give each other a hand with the clearing and the building."

"What do we do now?" asked Elizabeth.

"Well, Dick and I will be off in the morning. The rest of you can stay here in town until we've had a chance to find our land and to get some kind of shelter built. Then we'll come back and take you there."

10 THE LOYALIST LIST

The list is part of the original list of people who settled in Township No. 1 at Cataraqui in 1784. Try to find answers to the following questions:

1. According to this list how many people were settled in Township No. 1 on October 9, 1784? How many were adult men? Adult women? Children?
2. Which is the largest family on the list? Does this family have more children than any other? (Think carefully about this and read all the names.)
3. The remarks by the census-taker tell us a lot. Why were some of the settlers away? Does this tell you anything about what they were doing at home?
4. Were all the people living in Township No. 1 farmers? If not, what else did some of them do?
5. How big was the average Loyalist family?
6. What other information can you find in this list about life at Cataraqui in 1784?
7. What is a census? Why is it taken? Find a modern census list of your area. What does it tell you about the people who live near you?

This pioneer is sowing seed on the land he has cleared. Why has he left the stumps in the field? What kind of seed do you think he is planting?

On page 43 there are ten vertical columns of numbers. They represent the following statistics:

First column: **number of men**
Second column: **number of women**
Third column: **male children above 10**
Fourth column: **male children below 10**
Fifth column: **female children above 10**

Sixth column: **female children below 10**
Seventh column: **servants**
Eighth column: **total number of people**
Ninth column: **rations for each family**
Tenth column: **acres of land cleared**

LIST OF LOYALISTS AND DISBANDED SOLDIERS SETTLED IN TOWNSHIP NO. 1, CATARAQUI

9th Day of October, 1784

Description											Remarks
Michael Grass	1	1	3		3	1		9	8½	10	
Eman Ellerbeck	1	1		1		1		4	3	4	Family in the States
William Atherson	1	1						2	2	2	Woman on the Land
Simon Swart	1							1	1		
Michael Taylor	1							1	1		
Aron Brouer	1	1						2	2	2	Woman on the Land
Elijah Grooms	1	1						2	2		
Chris Danby	1							1	1		
Matthew Vancoure	1							1	1		
Benjamin Vancoure	1	1						2	2		
Widow Wright		1						1	1		On the Land in the Back of the Concession
John Holmes	1	1		2	3			7	6	1½	Woman on the Land
Tsich Orser	1							1	1	3	
Solloman Orser	1	1						2	2		Woman on the Land
Arthur Orser	1	1	1					3	2½		
Gilbert Orser	1	1						2	2		
John Fadle	1							1	1		
Amos Ansley	1	1	1		1	1		5	4½		Family on their Land
Widow Orser		1	1	1	1			4	3½		
Silas Palmer	1							1	1		
George Wetlow	1							1	1		
Dan McGuin	1	1	1			1		4	3½		Family on their Land
Mich Money	1							1	1	2	Gone to Canada. Expected back this Fall
John Monair	1	1			1			3	3	3	Woman Sick
William Bell	1							1	1		Gone into the States. Expected back this Fall
John Stringer	1	1				1		3	2½		Quitted his Land and gone off
William Boone	1							1	1		Gone into the States for Seed Wheat
Jacob Bestiedo	1	1	3	1				6	5½		Family on their Land; one Child dead since last Muster
Joseph Anderson	1	1	1	1				4	3½		Not yet come to their Land
John Warner	1							1	1		Employed at the King's Saw Mills
Robert Findle	1							1	1		Employed Engineer's Work
Fred Baker	1	1	2					4	4		Gone to Montreal for his Family
David Whiteman	1	1						2	2	4	Woman on the Land
George Gallaway	1	1						2	2		Gone to Oswegatiche for Cattle
John Cannon	1	1	1	1	1			5	4½		ditto

LIST OF SEEDS SENT BY MAJOR HOLLAND FOR THE USE OF SETTLERS IN THE UPPER COUNTRY

Quebec, 18th May, 1784

One bag containing	4 lb. of Onion Seed
One bag containing	11 lb. of Norfolk Turnip
One bag containing	9 lb. early Dutch Turnip
One bag containing	12 lb. large Dutch Cabbage
One bag containing	13 lb. Sellery Seed
One bag containing	17 lb. Orange Carrot
One bag containing	4 lb. Short-top Radish
One bag containing	3 lb. Parsley Seed
One bag containing	One bushel of Marrowfat Pease

One of the first tasks of the Loyalists was to build a cabin. Most of the cabins were built like this one, out of logs. Look carefully at this and at the other pictures. Try to write a set of instructions for someone who wants to build a cabin. What would have to be done first? What material would be used to make a roof? How would a fireplace and a chimney be built?

Rolling up the logs

Roof of basswood bark

Round logs

11
THE BARN RAISING

Elizabeth carefully balanced the kettle on the hot glowing coals in the fireplace. Using two pieces of wood as tongs, she lifted more hot coals onto the top of the kettle. "One more kettle of bread baking," she thought, "that should make enough for all the people who will come to the barn-raising and to the bee today."

The men were out in the clearing, notching and preparing logs. Inside the cabin, the women were hard at work too. Some were spinning the flax they had grown. Others were making deerskin hides into clothes for themselves and their families.

"Did you hear about poor Hannah Hoffmann?" one of them said. "She wanted to look all clean and pretty for her beau, who was coming in from the next concession. So she took her deerskin dress — the only one she had — and put it in the kettle to boil it clean. Well, you can imagine what happened. It shrank to a tiny strip. She couldn't wear it at all. Her family came home and found her huddled up in a blanket on the bed, not a thing to wear until she could make herself a new dress."

The women all broke into laughter. Elizabeth giggled. "Don't you be laughing, young lady," her mother said, smiling at her. "Soon enough Jake will be coming round here courting you, and it will be your turn to worry about how you look."

"He will not," Elizabeth blushed. "We're friends, that's all. I'm going down to see how the barn is coming." She stood up and ran out.

Outside, the children were playing. Elizabeth waved at her younger sister and brother and Jake's brother Samuel as she walked across the clearing.

The men were hard at work on the huge pile of logs for the barn. Richard Booth and Hans Vandersteen, a farmer from the next concession, carried a long, heavy log to the stone foundation that had already been laid.

"How's it going?" Elizabeth shouted to her father.

"Fine! We'll be done well before nightfall. We're coming in for dinner pretty soon. You'd better go and tell your mother to get the food on the table."

Elizabeth ran back. Her mother had taken the freshly baked bread from the kettle. She filled the kettle with water and hung it over a fire outside the cabin.

"The men are coming in a minute. I'll make the tea," said Elizabeth. She took several handsful of dried peppermint leaves and threw them into the steaming water.

Her mother was laying out food on the split log they used as a dinner table. There was salt pork and a pot of pea soup. Mrs. McDonnell had made a fish pie from boiled fish and potatoes, and had topped it with a thick pastry crust. There was the bread Elizabeth had baked that morning, sliced dried pumpkin, and heaps of blackberries, picked the day before by Elizabeth's brother and sister.

The men came in but didn't stay long. They ate and went back to work.

Raising the barn walls and adding the roof took all afternoon. At six o'clock, everyone was back again, tired and hungry. For supper, there was more salt pork and a shoulder of venison, fried corn porridge and maple sugar. Elizabeth made "coffee", using dried corn and barley.

Her father brought out some spruce beer and soon the clearing rang with the sound of laughter and loud voices. One of the men produced a bottle of rum and passed it around the circle.

"Cornelius," shouted one of the men, "did you bring your fiddle? Let's get over there and give that barn a good christening."

Soon fiddle music bounced off the walls of the new barn. The men and women whirled around, dancing jigs and reels. The smaller children soon fell asleep, their heads pillowed on piles of straw.

Jake and Elizabeth were tired of dancing. "Let's go for a walk," Jake suggested.

They walked out of the barn, and sat down on a large flat rock nearby. "One day," Jake said, "one day, I'm going to have a great big farm with cows and horses and oxen and pigs. And I'll build a big house from sawn lumber, not a log cabin, but a house like the one we used to have back home. There will be real glass in the windows and the floors will be made from wood instead of dirt. And we'll have real furniture, made by a carpenter."

"And I'll have pretty dresses, just like the ones my mother had to leave behind," sighed Elizabeth. "I'll have a wagon pulled by two grey horses, and there will be real roads to drive on, not just paths like we have now. I'll go to town once a month and bring home silk and laces for dresses for my children. And my house will have rooms for everyone who comes to visit."

They sat quietly on the rock. The fiddling had stopped and people began to pour out of the barn. "Time to go home," yelled Richard Booth. Jake and Elizabeth climbed down from their rock and hurried back to the new barn.

1. It was fairly easy to put the lower logs for the McDonnell barn into place. It was not so easy to place the higher ones. How did the men raise the logs to the top of the barn walls? What do you think the roof was made of?
2. Why didn't the McDonnells use real tea and coffee? Find out what was used in their place in pioneer days.
3. Make a list of the food the people ate at the barn-raising. What kinds of crops would they have to grow to make these dishes? What animals would they have to raise? Did they eat anything that did not come from the farm?
4. Draw a picture of the men at work on the barn, or of the women spinning flax. What is flax? What kind of cloth is made from it?
5. What is a "bee"? Suggest some things early pioneers found easier to do as a group than by themselves. Do people hold bees now?

RECIPES:

Salt Pork:

For 200 lb. meat, take 14 lbs. salt, ¹/₂ lb. saltpetre, 2 qts. molasses and 1 pt. beer; mix with enough water to dissolve the salt. Bring mixture to the boil. Remove scum. Cool. Pour salt liquid over pork and leave the meat in this brine for six to eight weeks, turning and basting it every two to three days. Remove pork from brine. Lay on rack to dry or smoke in smokehouse.

Steamed Corn Bread:

Take three cups of cornmeal and one cup of flour. Scald two cups of the meal with boiling water. Add the other cup of meal and the flour, two cups of sour milk, one cup molasses, one teaspoon soda, and a little salt. Steam three hours.

Indian Mush:

Put water in a kettle and hang over fire to boil with a little salt. Stir in cornmeal handful by handful. Cook as long as possible while thin before adding the final handful of cornmeal to thicken the whole mixture. If desired to be fried: turn into a dish and set to cool. Cut in slices and fry on a hot pan.

Spruce Beer:

Take seven pounds of spruce wood and boil it until the bark peels off. Take the spruce out of the kettle and pour in three gallons of molasses. Boil again, taking off the scum as the mixture boils. Cool. Stir in a pint of yeast and mix well. Put the mixture in a barrel and let it work for two to three days.

Dried Apples:

"First they don't take half the peeling off,
Then on some dirty cord they're strung,
Then from some chamber window hung;
Where they serve as roosts for flies
Until they're ready to make pies."

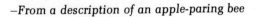
—From a description of an apple-paring bee

12 THE HUNGRY YEAR

Richard Booth stormed angrily into his cabin. "Nothing," he shouted, "nothing at all. I've been to see every farmer on this concession and nobody has any food to sell. They tell me it's just as bad in town. Not a loaf of bread for sale, no matter how much you offer for it.

"There's not a soul in this whole township—and hardly anyone all the way down to Quebec—who raised a decent crop this year. They're calling it the Hungry Year; nobody has enough to eat. Not a drop of rain from June to August. Now it's December and almost everything we had stored, is gone. Not a head of wheat left and scarcely an ear of corn.

"And now the government has stopped our rations. I know they told us they'd feed us for just three years, but who expected this? I could have had a crop big enough to feed three families if the rain had come. Now I've got nothing. Don't they know what's happening out here? We're starving and nobody cares."

Mary Booth looked up; she was stirring a beef bone in a pot of water to make soup. "Don't shout so. It doesn't make things better. We'll get through somehow."

"How? How many times have you used that same bone for soup? Three times, four times? And what else have we got to eat? A few potatoes, a little salt pork? The last of the cornmeal?

"The children are skin and bones and we're little better. Jake," he said, "go down to the stream. Maybe you can break the ice and find us a fish. You're old enough to do your part."

Richard grabbed his rifle from the wall. "I'm going out to find us something to eat. Not a deer left in these parts, but maybe I can find a pigeon, or a sparrow." He stomped out of the cabin.

Mary Booth sighed. "Go on, Jake. And take Sammy with you. He needs some fresh air."

Jake took his forked fishing stick off the wall and the two boys walked along the path toward the frozen stream. Jake smashed the ice with a large rock. He saw a dark shape move slowly along the bottom of the stream. He lunged at it and the fish was caught in the fork of his stick. Jake slowly edged it up the side of the stream, ready to catch it with his hands.

Sammy, who had been leaning over the side of the hole, suddenly slipped on the ice. With a scream, he tumbled into the freezing water, and fell against the stick. The fish escaped.

Jake grabbed Sammy, to pull him out of the water. His brother's skin was turning blue and he shivered wildly. Jake picked him up and ran back to the house with him. "Mom," he yelled, "Sammy fell into the water!"

When Richard Booth came home at night, Sammy was in bed, covered with thick blankets. "There was nothing to shoot," said Booth, putting the rifle back in its place. "It will have to be cornmeal and water again for supper tonight. What happened to Sammy?"

"He fell into the stream; I'm trying to keep him warm, but he's so thin. Richard, I'm worried about him," said his wife.

"Haven't you got any medicine?"

"I'm brewing some wormwood tea. Maybe it will help. I don't know."

Sammy was no better the next morning. "I'm going into Kingston," Jake's father announced. "That child needs food. I'll get us something even if it kills me."

He wasn't back by nightfall. As dawn came, Jake was woken up by his mother's crying. She was bent over Sammy's bed. "Mom," he asked, "Mom, what's wrong?"

She turned to him for a moment. "Your brother's dead," she said.

Jake went out to meet his father on the path. He waited till noon. Then he saw him; his hands were empty. "Nothing," his father said, "not a scrap of food to buy in town."

Jake suddenly broke down. "Dad," he sobbed, "Dad, Sammy's dead."

His father put his arms around him. He was silent for a minute, then he said, "this country, this hellish country! We'd have been better off in a Yankee prison!"

The next day, Richard Booth made a rough coffin for his son. He went into the woods behind the cabin to dig a grave.

All the neighbors came for the funeral. "There's no preacher here, so I'll say the words for you," Simon McDonnell announced. He took an old Bible from under his coat and began to read. The others bowed their heads.

"Yea, though I walk through the valley of the shadow of death, I will fear no evil, for thou art with me: thy rod and thy staff, they comfort me...."

When McDonnell had finished reading, the neighbors placed the coffin in the grave and began to fill in the earth. Mary Booth began to cry. The women led her back to the cabin and the group sat down in silence.

"I hear Tompkins, over in the next concession, has given up and has gone back to the States," one man said, at last. "Must be twenty farmers in this township alone have gone back south this year. Better than starving. Maybe we all should go."

Mary Booth lifted her head. "We're not leaving. I've given three years and one son to this land. I'm going to stay until I see good crops growing and a fine house on this land. Maybe I won't live to see the day that this new land gives us everything the old one did, but Jake will. I am not giving up now."

SOME PIONEER CURES FOR SICKNESS

Sickness:	Cure:
Coughs	Syrup made from roots of spignet
Stomach-ache	Catnip tea
Physical condition requiring a general tonic	Tansy tea
Indigestion	Hop tea, dried burdock root tea
Poor blood	Cherry bark tea
Burns	Black elder, lard resin and beeswax, mixed into a salve
Bruises and swellings	Smartweed steeped in vinegar
Lame feet	Poultice made from plantain leaves
Abrasions, open sores	Bean leaves heated with lard. Pour off lard and cool mixture
Sore throat	Mandrake root tea for gargle
Bad nerves	Chew roots of nerve vine
Open wounds	Roots of elecampane tea
Whooping cough	Roots of elecampane syrup Hog's lard and garlic. Rub mixture on the backbone, the soles of the feet and on the hands. Use every night before going to bed
Colds	Spearmint tea, infusion of mullein, roots of spignet syrup
All sicknesses, where other cures have failed	Wormwood tea

1. When Samuel fell sick, why didn't the Booths call a doctor?

2. What is a preacher? Why was there no preacher at Samuel's funeral? Why didn't the Booths bury Samuel in a cemetery?

3. Imagine you are lost in the woods and have nothing to eat. What would you do? Write a paragraph describing where and how you would look for food.

The list shows some ways early settlers, such as the Loyalists, tried to cure sickness. Do you understand all the cures? If not, find out what they are. Collect some of the plants named if you can, and prepare them for use. Make a list of things we use today to cure the sicknesses named in the list. Do you think they are better than the ones the Loyalists used? Why or why not? Why didn't they use the same cures we use today?

13 THE GRIST MILL

The government gave the Loyalists grain supplies during their first three years in Canada. Wheat and corn were among their first crops. The wheat had to be turned into flour and the corn into meal, so that the settlers could use them.

The hand mills they received from the government to grind the wheat and corn did not work too well. Instead, the Loyalists borrowed an idea from the Indians. They used what they called plumping mills or hominy blocks. These blocks were made by carefully burning out the inside of a hardwood stump. With a long-handled pestle, the grain was then crushed in the hollow stump. This method worked well for corn or wild rice but was not good enough for grinding wheat.

Soldiers had begun to build a grist mill on the Cataraqui River even before the Loyalists arrived at Cataraqui. It was the only mill between the Bay of Quinte and Cornwall. Many farmers came by boat and on foot, carrying their grain in sacks, to have it ground. The trip sometimes took as long as two weeks. Because so many used the mill, each farmer might have had to wait up to three weeks for his turn. Then he would go home with his bags of flour.

The Cataraqui mill, built beside a waterfall, was powered by a wheel. The water from the fall ran along a wooden trough, called a mill race, onto the wheel blades. This turned the waterwheel and caused the shaft and the gears to turn inside the mill.

There were two millstones in the grist mill. One, set into the floor, did not turn; the other, attached to a tall shaft, turned. As this top stone moved against the steady bottom stone, the grain poured from a hopper onto the surfaces of the millstones, and was crushed and ground into flour.

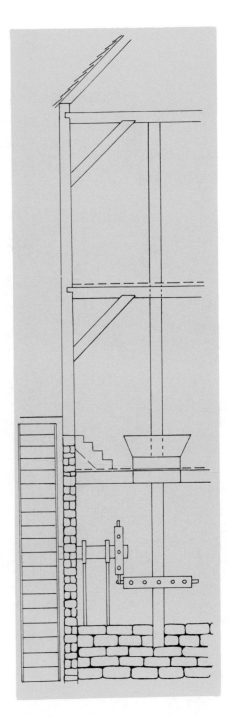

These pioneers are grinding corn into meal using a hominy block. Does this look like hard work? How long do you think it would take to grind enough corn to fill the bucket?

1. Imagine you are either Richard Booth or Simon McDonnell. The two of you have made the trip to the mill. Describe your journey, your wait and how your grain was ground. How would you get to the Cataraqui River and home again? What would you eat? What would you talk about with other farmers who were also waiting at the mill?

2. Why is it necessary to have grain milled into flour? Why can't you eat the wheat straight from the field? Make a chart tracing the steps from the time the wheat is planted to the time it appears on your table as a loaf of bread.

3. Find out how grain is milled today. Is cornmeal still used today? If so, what for? Find a recipe that uses cornmeal.

The Glenora Mill was built in 1794 by Major Peter Van Alstine, a Loyalist who came from Kenderhook, N.Y. This mill was the earliest in Prince Edward County and used water from a lake on a mountain above Glenora.

14 THE WEDDING

Elizabeth closed the door of the McDonnell's clapboard house behind her. It was barely dawn. Only the song of the birds broke the silence as she walked across the clearing to the rock where she and Jake had sat many years ago.

She raised her skirts and sat down. Today she would become Mrs. Jacob Booth. Jake, his father and some of the neighbors had built a fine new clapboard house for them on land Jake had bought three miles away. After the wedding they would live there.

Chin in hand, she thought about the ten years that had passed since she came to Canada. She tried to remember her old home in the United States. Ten years ago, she and Jake had dreamed about a house and a carriage and a good farm. Now they were about to begin their married life with all those things.

Her father came out of the house and walked over to her. "Sad?" he asked. "Sad on your wedding day?"

"No, just thinking about growing up here and the hard times you and Mother have had. Now Jake and I are starting out, just like you and Mother did more than twenty years ago. Were you ever sorry you left Vermont, Dad?"

"Oh, aye, that we were. There were times when I thought we'd turn around and go right back. But it's easier now and will be even better for you and Jake. We've made a living from this land and it's a good land."

The two stayed together for a moment, in silence.

"What! Sitting out there doing nothing?" Anne McDonnell called from the door of the house. "You can't loaf on your wedding day, my girl! The guests will be here in a few hours and they'll be wanting food and drink. And there's a few stitches to go into the hem of your dress yet."

Elizabeth laughed. She ran back to the house and went to her room. She carefully lifted her wedding dress from the bed. It was the same dress her mother had been married in and had brought with her in the McDonnell's iron trunk. The silk had yellowed slightly with age, but the lace still stood up stiffly around the sleeves and the skirt. Elizabeth and her mother had spent many evenings altering the dress to fit.

Out in the yard, the Booths had arrived. Jake looked ill at ease in the new suit his father had bought for him in Kingston. He kept tugging at the sleeves of the jacket.

The preacher, in his long black coat and black hat, had come on horseback. He dismounted and took the Bible from his coat pocket.

The guests fell silent. Elizabeth put her hand on her father's arm and together they walked out into the sunshine. In front of the preacher, she stopped, turned to Jake and smiled. They joined hands and waited for the wedding ceremony to begin.

1. Much had changed on the McDonnell's farm between the time of the barn-raising and the wedding. Make a list of all the things that might have changed in the ten years. Do you think the McDonnell's served the same food at the wedding as they did at the barn-raising? If not, make up a menu for the wedding supper.

2. Where do you think the preacher came from for the ceremony? Why wasn't the wedding held at a church?

3. The story tells what Elizabeth did on her wedding day. What do you think Jake did? Write a paragraph describing the thoughts he may have had.

15 FROM LOG CABIN TO CLAPBOARD HOUSE

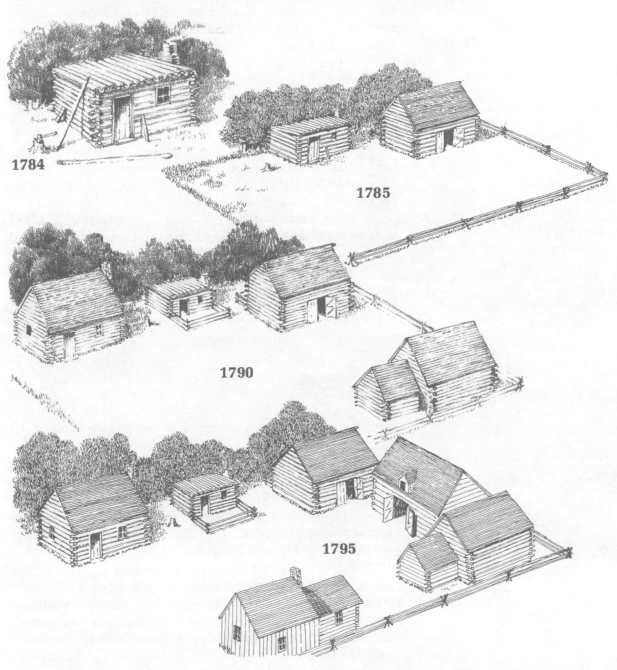

1784

1785

1790

1795

1810

These pictures show the McDonnell farm through the years: as it was in 1784 when the Loyalists arrived at Cataraqui; in 1785, the year of the barn-raising; in 1790, three years after the Hungry Year; in 1795 when Jake and Elizabeth got married and in 1810, when many other changes had taken place.

Make a chart showing these changes. Put the dates of the pictures in one column. In the next, you could list the buildings you see in each picture. Write down what each building was used for. Make other columns in your chart that show the kind of materials used and what advantages each new building had over the one before it.

What else would you like to put on your chart? You could write a letter Mrs. McDonnell might have sent to a relative in Vermont, describing her 25 years in Canada. Or, you might draw a picture that shows what you think the McDonnell farm looked like in 1850.

16 THE GROWTH OF KINGSTON

Kingston in 1792

Kingston in 1828

Kingston in 1832

**WAGES PAID IN
KINGSTON IN 1820**

	£	s	d
To a blacksmith, per day	0	7	8
To a blacksmith, per month	5	14	0
To a mason, per day	0	8	4
To a carpenter, per day	0	7	9
To a common laborer, per annum	28	16	0
per winter month	2	3	3
per summer month	3	5	2
per day, in harvest	0	5	2
Women for housework, per week	0	5	6
Spinning, generally 1 s more			
Cost of clearing and fencing			
five acres of wild land	19	4	0

**PRICES CURRENT IN
THE KINGSTON
MARKET IN 1820**

	£	s	d
Beef, per lb.	0	0	7
Mutton, per lb.	0	0	7
Veal, per lb.	0	0	7½
Pork, per lb.	0	0	10
Fowls, per pair	0	4	0
Cheese, per lb.	0	0	7½
Cheese, per doz.	0	0	10
Butter, per lb.	0	1	3
Butter, per doz.	0	1	1¼
Eggs, per doz.	0	1	3
Peas, per bushel	0	6	0
Potatoes, per bushel	0	2	6
Oats, per bushel	0	3	9
Turnips, per bushel	0	1	3
Cabbages, per head	0	0	2
Flour, per cwt.	0	16	3
Flour, per bbl.	1	10	0
Tallow, per lb.	0	0	8
Wool, per lb.	0	2	5
Hay, per ton	2	0	0
Straw, per bundle	0	0	3
Wood, per cord	0	12	6
Lime, per bushel	0	1	0
A good work horse	15	11	0
A good cow	5	5	0
An ox	8	16	0
A sheep	0	14	3

17 THE LATER IMMIGRANTS

BAY OF QUINTY.

18 45

STEAM PACKET

PRINCE EDWARD,

CAPTAIN BONTER,

WILL UNTIL FURTHER NOTICE PLY ON THE BAY OF QUINTY, ON THE FOLLOWING DAYS:

Upwards from Kingston at six o'clock P. M. on *SUNDAY, TUESDAY, & THURSDAY*

Downwards from the Head of the Bay, at 5 o'clock, P. M. on *MONDAY, WEDNESDAY, & FRIDAY,*

And will touch for freight and passengers at all intermediate Ports.

The proprietor having a Warehouse at his command at Belleville, will store all goods *free of Warehouse charges that are shipped by the Prince Edward.*

☞ *Clergymen* of all denominations will as usual, have their passages *free.*

This picture is of Simpson's Tavern in Belleville, Upper Canada, built five years after the first Loyalists arrived.

This early stagecoach ran between Kingston and York. Why is it on runners instead of wheels? What is York called today?

A view of King Street, in Kingston, painted in 1833. How do you think King Street has changed since this picture was painted?

THE WORDS

ammunition bullets or gunpowder used in a gun

auger a tool for making holes in wood

barley a type of grain used for food

bateau a flat-bottomed river boat with oars or sails or both

brine very salty water, good for keeping food from going bad

census a count of the people in the area

chisel a cutting tool with a sharp edge at the end of its blade

clapboard thin board, thicker along one edge than along the other, used to cover buildings

colonist a person who leaves one country to settle in another country where few people live

cornmeal ground up corn

coulter a sharp blade on a plow

delegate a person chosen by a group of people to speak and act for them

flax a type of plant. Linen is made from the stems of the flax plant.

frontier the furthest part of a settled country, where the wilds begin

frow a tool used for cutting shakes, a type of roof covering made from wood

gimblet a small tool used for boring holes

gouge a chisel used for cutting grooves or holes

grindstone a flat round stone used to grind grain or sharpen tools

grist mill a place where grain is ground into flour

harrow a heavy frame used to break up clods of earth in a plowed field

independent not depending on anyone else; if a country is independent, its people make their own laws and are not governed by anyone else.

loyal faithful to one's king or government

merchant a person who buys and sells things

missionary a person who tells other people about his or her religion, and tries to convince them to believe what he or she believes.

molasses a sweet syrup made from sugar cane

notching cutting V-shaped nicks into something

pestle a tool for crushing things into powder

pioneer a person who goes to live in a place where very few people have lived before

plow a piece of farm machinery that turns over the soil

preacher a minister

proclamation a public announcement; a notice presented to the people

rations a limited amount of food given out in times when food is scarce

rebel someone who fights against authority

revolution the attempt to completely change a government, usually by force

saltpetre a mineral used as a fertilizer or in making gunpowder

sawmill a mill where logs are sawn into boards

scald heat almost to boiling

scythe a long, curved blade used for cutting grass

seigneury a piece of land given by the King of France to someone in New France

shingles thin pieces of wood or other material used to cover a roof

slave a person who is owned by another person

smallpox a fatal disease which spreads quickly; many people used to die from smallpox

tax money people pay to the government for services, such as roads

treaty an agreement, usually written, between two countries or groups of people

tribe a group of people united by race under the same leaders

venison the meat of deer

wedge a piece of wood or metal used to help split something, such as another piece of wood

wharf a platform built out from shore where ships can dock

yeast a material that helps bread or cakes to rise